DOABLE TWELFTH NIGHT

DOABLE TWELFTH NIGHT

Copyright © 2020 Brent N. Von Horn

All rights reserved. Printed in the United States of America. No part of this book may be used or reproduced in any manner whatsoever without written permission except in the case of brief quotations embodied in critical articles or reviews.

This work may be performed before live audiences, provided a license to do so is obtained from Brent N. Von Horn prior to performance. See detailed information on how to obtain such license at the back of this book, or contact the author at:

Nautic Publishing

Brent N. Von Horn

https://www.nauticproductions.com

Cover design by Nautic Productions © 2020 Brent N. Von Horn

ISBN: 978-1-7349239-4-0 (Paperback); 978-1-7349239-5-7 (Ebook)

First Edition, 2020

10 9 8 7 6 5 4 3 2 1

DOABLE TWELFTH NIGHT

**William Shakespeare's Play
In "Do Able" Form**

by

Brent Nautic Von Horn

CONTENTS:

Introduction 3
Synopsis... 5
Characters 7
PROLOGUE 1
ACT 1 2
ACT 2 30
ACT 3 57
ACT 4 89
ACT 5 105
EPILOGUE 122
Character Notes... 123
Set Design Notes 131
Production License 133

Introduction

William Shakespeare is often revered as the Greatest Playwright ever. However, he lived 400 years ago and in modern times actors and audiences both have trouble understanding him. These "Do Able" versions of Shakespeare's plays are true versions of his works, still using the Bard's words, but edited to be more easily comprehensible.

Believe it or not, there are some who say there was no such person as William Shakespeare, that he was made up as the pseudonym of some other writer. There is little in the historical record to document the life of William Shakespeare. It could be possible that some educated member of high society wrote under the name of "William Shakespeare" to avoid the scandal of being associated with theatre. His plays were written in the years when bubonic plague epidemics ravaged London, and theatres were dirty places. The "players" who acted were all men, by law, as the stage was not considered suitable for women. Whoever Shakespeare was, he wrote for the audiences of his time. He wrote for the low-browed, uneducated, illiterate masses, who wanted action, sex, bawdy insults and scandalous subject matter. In the same plays, he also wrote for the high-brow elite, the educated and cultured top tier of his society, who appreciated poetry, love and tales of honor.

The goals of this Do Able version remain the same, aiming at the right balance of both fun and art. For actors, plotlines are explained, character breakdowns are provided, and stage directions (not written down in Shakespeare's time) are provided. For audiences, the original text is adapted, to make it more palatable to modern ears, while still retaining the magic and beauty of Shakespeare's writing. This means, largely, the cutting of some minor characters, as well as many lines of dialogue where (measured by our short attention span culture) Shakespeare perhaps waxed a bit too poetic and strayed away from his plotlines and action.

Yet, enough remains to be true to the original. If we've succeeded in writing this book, you will need nothing else in order to perform an outstanding production of William Shakespeare's *Twelfth Night (or What You Will)* with more clarity and effect than ever before.

Synopsis

The jester (Feste) leads us through this romp of a comedy.

Duke Orsino is desperately in love with a woman (the Countess Olivia) who will have nothing to do with him. He sends messengers to plead his case: first Valentine, who doesn't get far; next Cesario who does such a good job wooing for the Duke that Olivia falls in love instead with Cesario. Oops.

But we know Olivia's love is misplaced. We know that Cesario is actually a woman, Viola, who survived the shipwreck that killed everyone else aboard, including her twin brother, Sebastian. Poor Viola disguised herself as a man in order to hide in Duke Orsino's employment while she tries to figure out what to do with her life.

Viola finds herself falling in love with Duke Orsino, but she's unable to profess her love since he sees her as a boy. Meanwhile, she rejects Olivia's love.

In Olivia's house lives her cousin, Sir Toby, a drunkard who has invited his friend, Sir Andrew, to come woo Olivia so that he can freeload off of Sir Andrew's money. Also there are Maria, Olivia's waiting gentlewoman, and Olivia's stuck up butler, Malvolio. Maria is amused by Sir

Toby's drunken humor, but Malvolio is not; they hatch a prank, to put Malvolio in his place by making it seem he is mad.

Sebastian, it turns out, did not drown. He was also rescued, and comes to town where Olivia is thrilled to have him respond to her love; they get married.

Sir Toby also tricks his friend, Sir Andrew, into a farce duel with Viola, while she's pretending to be a man. But that backfires horribly, because it is Sebastian who answers the challenge.

Duke Orsino finally decides to visit Olivia in person, but he is shocked to hear her say that she married his messenger (Viola). Viola is just as shocked. The Duke, enraged, decides to kill Viola. Fortunately, Sebastian shows up and all are amazed that there are two twins.

Instead of killing Viola, the Duke marries her. Sir Toby and Maria are also wed. It's a very happy ending.

Feste leads the whole cast in a fun song at the end.

Characters

VIOLA	A lady of Messaline
SEBASTIAN	Viola's twin brother
DUKE ORSINO	Duke (Count) of Illyria
CURIO	]
VALENTINE	] gentlemen serving Orsino
OLIVIA	an Illyrian Countess
FESTE	Olivia's jester
MALVOLIO	Olivia's butler
MARIA	gentlewoman serving Olivia
SIR TOBY	Olivia's uncle
SIR ANDREW	Sir Toby's friend
CAPTAIN	sea captain who rescues Viola
ANTONIO	sea captain who rescues Sebastian
FIRST OFFICER	
SECOND OFFICER	] policemen
EXTRAS:	Musicians, Lords, Fishermen, Attendants

TWELFTH NIGHT

or What You Will

PROLOGUE

Enter Feste.

FESTE
Mayhap you've come to watch us play this play;
in truth, I hope so, else you've gone astray!
Misgendered and misidentified be we,
from vile creatures coughed up by the stormy sea,
to drunkards and inexplicitly dense men.
I give you now what you may take away then:
nothing but frivolity, pure and simple. –
We start in far off country: Illyria –
far off enough!
We begin, as ev'rything begins: with love.
Now clap you me, and again at the end, when I tell thee!
(Feste exits.)

ACT 1

SCENE 1

Duke Orsino's palace.

Musicians play.

Enter Duke Orsino, Curio, and other Lords.

DUKE ORSINO
If music be the food of love, play on.
Oh, when my eyes did see Olivia first,
methought she purged the air of pestilence!
That instant was I turned into a stag,
leaping through fields of brightly colored hay,
and my desires, like fell and cruel hounds
e'er since pursue me.

CURIO
You were, my lord, turned into a leaping hart?

DUKE ORSINO
Quite so, dear Curio, quite so, but now
'tis my beating heart that leaps for her love.

(Enter Valentine.)

DUKE ORSINO
How now! What news from her?

VALENTINE
So please my lord, I was inside not allowed,
but from her handmaid do return this answer:
Lady Olivia, thy heart's true goal,
in mourning is, and shall remain seven years.
She hides herself 'neath heavy veils and cries
all day, all night, with eye-offending brine,
all this to season a brother's dead love.

DUKE ORSINO
Thou deliverest my flowers? My notes?
My candy? My pasta ravioli, and my love?

VALENTINE
Aye, my lord, to handmaiden's hand,
but thee thyself I'm told from handmaiden's lips,
may not, wilt not, thy Lady's love receive.

DUKE ORSINO
Oh, darn.

(They exit.)

SCENE 2

Beach.

Enter Viola, a Captain and fishermen with nets.

VIOLA
What country, friends, is this?

CAPTAIN
This is Illyria, lady. Dry land,
and friendly for your waterloggèd feet.

VIOLA
Illyria? I know it not, but as
a name upon a map, along our ship's path.
And what should I do in Illyria?
My brother, he was aboard our ship,
and parted in the vilest storm were we.
Perchance he is not drown'd; what think you, fishers?

FISHERMEN
'Twas nasty storm of yesternight.
'Twas perchance that you yourself were saved.
'Twas no one but you yourself on beach today.

VIOLA
Oh, poor brother! Asleep in a deep blue tomb!

CAPTAIN
Likely true, madam; there's no sign that any
but thee survived thy ship's downing at sea.
But holdfast to hope thy might, for the sea
is fickle beast, full of mystery, and
indeed threw thee ashore in blessings be.

VIOLA
Know'st thou this country?

CAPTAIN
Aye, madam, well; for I was bred and born
not three hours' travel from this very place.

VIOLA
Who governs here?

CAPTAIN
A noble duke, in nature as in name.

VIOLA
What is the name?

CAPTAIN
Orsino.

VIOLA
Orsino! I have heard my father name him.
He was a bachelor, then.

CAPTAIN
And so is now,

though now 'tis fresh in murmur, -- as, you know,
what great ones do the less will prattle of, --
that he doth seek the love of fair Olivia.

VIOLA

What's she?

CAPTAIN

A virtuous maid, the daughter of a count
that died some twelvemonth since, then leaving her
in the protection of his son, her brother,
who shortly also died: for whose dear love,
they say, she hath abjured the company
and sight of men.

VIOLA

Oh, that I served that lady and might not be
discovered to the world, till I have made
mine own occasion mellow!

CAPTAIN

That would be hard to bring about,
because she will admit no kind of suit;
no, not even the duke's.

VIOLA

There is a fair behavior in thee, Captain;
I believe thou hast a mind that suits
within this fair and outward character.
I prithee, and I'll pay thee bounteously,

conceal me what I am, and be my aide
for such disguise as haply shall become
the form of this intent. I'll serve this duke,
this fine and fair Orsino, who governs here.
Thou shall present me as a eunuch to him.
I shall so pass with ease, for I can sing
and speak to him in many sorts of music
that will allow me very worth his service.
What else may hap to time I will commit;
only shape thou thy silence to my wit.

CAPTAIN
Be you his eunuch, and your mute I'll be;
when my tongue blabs, then let my eyes not see.

VIOLA
I thank thee. Lead me on.

(They exit.)

SCENE 3

Olivia's house.

Enter Sir Toby and Maria.

SIR TOBY
What a plague means my niece, to take the death of her brother thus? I am sure care's an enemy to life.

Act 1 Scene 3

MARIA

By my troth, Sir Toby, you must come in earlier o' nights. Your cousin, my lady, takes great exceptions to your ill hours and too, begs you to confine yourself within the modest limits of order.

SIR TOBY

Confine! I'll confine myself no finer than I am; these clothes are good enough to drink in; and so be
these boots, too; an they be not, let them hang themselves in their own straps.

MARIA

That quaffing and drinking will undo you; I heard my lady talk of it yesterday, and of a foolish knight that you brought in one night here to be her wooer.

SIR TOBY

Who, Sir Andrew Aguecheek?

MARIA

Aye, he.

SIR TOBY

He's as tall a man as any's in Illyria.

MARIA

What's that to the purpose?

Act 1 Scene 3

SIR TOBY
Why, he has three thousand ducats a year.

MARIA
That may be, for now, but he's a very fool
and a prodigal.

SIR TOBY
Fie! He speaks three or four languages clear,
and hath all the good gifts of nature.

MARIA
He hath indeed, almost natural; but besides that
he's a fool, he's a great quarreler, and 'tis said
he hath the gift of a coward to allay the gust he
hath in quarrelling. 'Tis thought among the prudent
he would quickly have the gift of grave.

SIR TOBY
By this hand, they are scoundrels and subtractors
that say so of him. Who are they?

MARIA
They that add, moreover, he's drunk nightly in
your company.

SIR TOBY
With drinking healths to my niece!
I'll drink to her as long as there is passage
in my throat and drink in Illyria – Ho!

Act 1 Scene 3

(Enter Sir Andrew.)

SIR ANDREW
Sir Toby Belch! How now, Sir Toby Belch?

SIR TOBY
Sweet Sir Andrew Aguecheek!

SIR ANDREW
(To Maria.)
Bless you, fair shrew.

MARIA
And you too, sir.

SIR TOBY
Accost, Sir Andrew, accost.

SIR ANDREW
What's that?

SIR TOBY
My niece's chambermaid.

SIR ANDREW
Good Mistress Accost –

MARIA
My name is Mary, sir.

Act 1 Scene 3

SIR ANDREW
Good Mistress Mary Accost –

SIR TOBY
You mistake, knight; "accost" means front her, board her, woo her, assail her.

SIR ANDREW
By my troth, I would not do her in this company. Is that the meaning of "accost"?

MARIA
Fare you well, gentlemen.

(She exits.)

SIR TOBY
Oh, knight, when did I see thee so put down?

SIR ANDREW
Down I am, for feeling low and without hope.

SIR TOBY
Pourquoi my dear knight?

SIR ANDREW
What is "pourqui"? do or not do? I would I had bestowed that time in tongues that I have in fencing, dancing and bear-baiting. Oh, had I but followed the arts!

Act 1 Scene 3

SIR TOBY
Rest ye, and another bumper with thee.

SIR ANDREW
Faith, of course, another jot with thee, sir. But I'll home tomorrow, Sir Toby; your niece will not be seen; or if she be, it's four to one she'll none of me. The count himself here hard by woos her.

SIR TOBY
She'll none of the count: she'll not match above her degree, neither in estate, years, nor wit; I have heard her swear't. Tut, there's life in't, man.

SIR ANDREW
I'll stay a month longer. Shall we now drink more?

SIR TOBY
What shall we do else?

(They exit.)

SCENE 4

Enter Valentine and Viola in man's attire.

VALENTINE
You've been here but three weeks, Cesario,
and already hath the duke favored you.

VIOLA
Is the duke's favor constant, thinkest thou?

VALENTINE
No, believe me.

VIOLA
I thank you. Here comes the duke.

(Enter Duke Orsino, Curio and Attendants.)

DUKE ORSINO
Ho there, my fine good youth, Cesario;
thou know'st no less but all; I have unclasp'd
to thee the book even of my secret soul.
Therefore, good youth, address thy gait unto her;
be not denied access, stand at her doors,
and tell them, there thy fixed foot shall grow
till thou have audience.

Act 1 Scene 4

VIOLA

Yet, my noble lord,
if she be so abandon'd to her sorrow
as it is spoke, she never will admit me.

DUKE ORSINO

Be clamorous and leap all civil bounds
rather than make unprofited return.

VIOLA

Say I do speak with her, my lord, what then?

DUKE ORSINO

Oh, then unfold the passion of my love!
Surprise her with discourse of my dear faith;
use your wits and make some handsome things up.
It shall become thee well to act my woes.
She will attend it better in thy youth
than coming from a gent of more grave aspect.

VIOLA

I think not so, my lord.

DUKE ORSINO

Dear lad, believe it;
for they shall yet belie thy happy years,
that say thou art a man. Diana's lip
is not more smooth and rubious; thy small pipe
is as the maiden's organ, shrill and sound,
and all is semblative a woman's part.
I know thy constellation is right apt

for this affair. Prosper well in this now,
and thou shalt live as freely as thy lord,
to call his fortunes thine.

VIOLA
I'll do my best
to woo your lady.
(aside)
Yet, I find unexpectedly that I
myself, whoe'er I woo, wouldst be the wife
of my dear lord, the fair good Duke Orsino.

(They exit.)

SCENE 5

Olivia's house.

Enter Maria and Feste.

FESTE
(aside)
Hello!

MARIA
Nay, either tell me where thou hast been, of late,
or I shall not to my lady make excuse,
and she shall hang thee for being absent.

Act 1 Scene 5

FESTE
Let her hang me: he that is well hung in this world need fear no further slight.

MARIA
How be you so bold in your foolery?

FESTE
Well, God give them wisdom that have it; and those that are fools, let them use their talents.

MARIA
Yet you will be hanged for thy long absence, or, to be turned away, is not that as good as hanging to you?

FESTE
Fear not, I don't.
If I had hope, thou wert as witty a piece of Eve's flesh as any in Illyria.

MARIA
Peace, you rogue, no more o' that. Here comes my lady. Make your excuse wisely, you had best.

(Maria exits.)

FESTE
Wits, don't fail me now, put me into good feeling!
"Better a witty fool, than a foolish wit."

Act 1 Scene 5

(Enter Olivia with Malvolio.)

FESTE
God bless thee, lady!

OLIVIA
Take the fool away.

FESTE
Do you not hear, fellows? Take away the lady.

OLIVIA
Sir, I bade them take away you.

FESTE
Misprision in the highest degree! Lady, cucullus non facit monochum. That's to say I wear not motley in my brain. Good Madonna, give me leave to prove you a fool.

OLIVIA
Can you do it?

FESTE
Dexterously, good madam.

OLIVIA
Make your proof.

FESTE
Good Madonna, why mournest thou?

Act 1 Scene 5

OLIVIA
Good fool, for my brother's death.

FESTE
I think his soul is in hell, Madonna.

OLIVIA
I know his soul is in heaven, fool.

FESTE
The more fool, Madonna, to mourn for your brother's soul being in heaven.
Take away the fool, gentlemen.

OLIVIA
What think you of this fool, Malvolio?
Doth he not mend?

MALVOLIO
Yes, and shall do, till infirmity shake him.
Dulled wits doth ever make the better fool.

FESTE
God send you, sir, a speedy infirmity, for the better increasing your folly! Sir Toby will be sworn that I am no fox; but he will not pass his word for two pence that you are no fool.

OLIVIA
Ha, ha! How say you that, Malvolio?

MALVOLIO
I marvel your ladyship takes delight
in such a barren rascal.

OLIVIA
Oh, you are sick of self-love, Malvolio.
There is no slander in an allowed fool,
for he doth nothing but rail at the world's ills.

FESTE
Now Mercury endue thee with his feet,
for thou hath speakest well of fools!

(Enter Maria.)

MARIA
Madam -- there is at the gate a young gentleman
who much desires to speak with you.

OLIVIA
From the Count Orsino, is it?

MARIA
I know not, madam; 'tis a fair young man.

OLIVIA
Who of my people hold him in delay?

MARIA
Sir Toby, madam, your kinsman.

Act 1 Scene 5

OLIVIA
Fetch him off, I pray you; he speaks nothing but
madman. Fie on him! Go you, Malvolio;
if it be a suit from the count, I am sick,
or not at home; what you will, to dismiss it.

(Exit Maria and Malvolio.)

OLIVIA
Now you see, sir, how your fooling grows old
and people dislike it.

FESTE
Thou hast spoken for us, Madonna, as if
thy eldest son should be a fool.

(Enter Sir Toby.)

OLIVIA
By mine honor, half drunk.
What is he at the gate, cousin?

SIR TOBY
A gentleman.

OLIVIA
A gentleman! What gentleman?

SIR TOBY
'Tis a gentleman here – a plague o' these
pickle-herring! How now, sot!

Act 1 Scene 5

FESTE
Good Sir Toby!

OLIVIA
Cousin, cousin, how have you come so early
by this lethargy?

SIR TOBY
Lechery! I defy lechery. There's one at the gate.

OLIVIA
Aye, marry, what is he?

SIR TOBY
Let him be the devil, an he will, I care not.

(He exits.)

OLIVIA
What's a drunken man like, fool?

FESTE
Like a drowned man, a fool and a mad man.
One draught above heat makes him a fool; the
second mads him; and the third drowns him
deep.

OLIVIA
Go sit and watch the fool, fool, lest he sink.

(Feste exits.

Malvolio enters.)

MALVOLIO
Madam, yond young fellow swears he will speak with
you. I told him you were sick; he takes on him
to understand so much, and therefore comes
to speak with you. I told him you were asleep;
he seems to have a foreknowledge of that too,
and therefore comes to speak with you. What is
to be said to him, lady? He's fortified
against any denial.

OLIVIA
Tell him he shall not speak with me.

MALVOLIO
Has been told so, and he says, he'll stand at your
door like a sheriff's post, and be the supporter to
a bench, but he'll speak with you.

OLIVIA
What kind o' man is he?

MALVOLIO
Why, of very ill manner; he'll speak with you
or not leave hence.

OLIVIA
Of what personage and years is he?

Act 1 Scene 5

MALVOLIO
Not yet old enough for a man, nor young
enough for a boy. He is, though, I must say,
very well favored.

OLIVIA
Let him approach. Call in my gentlewoman.

MALVOLIO
(off)
Gentlewoman, my lady calls.

(He exits, as Maria enters.)

OLIVIA
Give me my veil. Come, throw it over my face.
We'll once more hear Orsino's embassy.

(Enter Viola.)

VIOLA
The honorable lady of the house, which is she?

OLIVIA
Speak to me; I shall answer for her.
Your will?

VIOLA
Most radiant, exquisite and unmatchable
beauty, -- I pray you, tell me if this be the lady of
the house, for I never saw her. I would be
loath to cast away my speech, for besides that

it is excellently well penned, I have
taken great pains to con it. Good beauties,
let me sustain no scorn; I am very
capable to recite competently.

OLIVIA

Whence came you, sir?

VIOLA

I can say little more than I have studied,
and that question's out of my part.
Good gentle one, give me modest assurance
if you be the lady of the house, that
I may proceed in my speech.

OLIVIA

Are you a comedian?

VIOLA

No, my profound heart; and yet, by the very
fangs of malice I swear, I am not that I play.
Are you the lady of the house?

OLIVIA

If I do not usurp myself, I am.

VIOLA

Well done! But this is from my commission:
I will on with my speech in your praise, and then
show you the heart of my message.

OLIVIA
Come to what is important in't: I forgive you the praise.

VIOLA
Alas, I took great pains to study it, and 'tis poetical.

OLIVIA
It is more like to be feigned. I pray you,
keep it in. I heard you were saucy at
my gates and allowed your approach rather than
to wonder at you than to hear you out.
If you have reason, be brief: 'tis not that time
of month with me to bear a poet's dilly.

VIOLA
My lady, I understand.
I'll be brief, but for your single ears only.

OLIVIA
Give us this place alone; we will hear this divinity.

(Exit Maria and Attendants.)

OLIVIA
Now, sir, what is your text?

VIOLA
Good madam, let me see your face.

OLIVIA
Have you any commission from your lord to

Act 1 Scene 5

negotiate with my face? You are now out
of your text -- but we will draw the curtain and
show you the picture. –
(unveiling)
Look you, sir: is't not well done?

VIOLA
Excellently done, if God did all.

OLIVIA
'Tis natural, sir, all, as God did send.

VIOLA
'Tis beauty truly blent, and I see why
my lord and master loves you: oh, such love.

OLIVIA
How does he love me?

VIOLA
With adoration, fertile tears,
with groans that thunder love, with sighs of fire.

OLIVIA
Your lord does know my mind: I cannot love
him.
Yet I suppose him virtuous, know him noble,
of great estate, of fresh and stainless youth;
a gracious person: but yet I cannot love him;
he might have took his answer long ago.

Act 1 Scene 5

VIOLA
If I did love you in my master's flame,
in your denial I would find no sense;
I would not understand it.

OLIVIA
Then, what would you do?

VIOLA
Make me a willow cabin at your gate,
and sing you loud even in the dead of night;
no hurricane would'st prevent me, for I would
cry out "Olivia, Olivia!"
Till you should pity me!

OLIVIA
You might do much.
What is your parentage?

VIOLA
I am a gentleman.

OLIVIA
Get you to your lord.
I cannot love him: let him send no more.
Unless, perchance, you come to see me again,
to tell me how he takes it.

VIOLA
Thou knows how he takes it, how he suffers.
Oh, cruel and heartless withholder of joy,
farewell, fair cruelty.

Act 1 Scene 5

(Viola exits.)

OLIVIA
"I am a gentleman." I'll be sworn thou art;
thy tongue, thy face, thy limbs, actions and spirit,
do give thee five-fold the grace of another.
Even so quickly may one catch the plague?
Methinks I feel this youth's perfections
with an invisible and subtle stealth
to creep in at mine eyes. Well, let it be.
What ho, Malvolio!

(Enter Malvolio.)

MALVOLIO
Here, madam, at your service.

OLIVIA
Run after that same peevish messenger,
the county's man: he left this ring behind him,
would I or not. Tell him I'll none of it.
Desire him to come this way tomorrow,
I'll give him reasons for't: hie thee, Malvolio.

MALVOLIO
Madam, I will.

(He exits.)

Act 1 Scene 5

>   OLIVIA
> I do not know in truth why I've done this now,
> and fear to find mine eye too great a flatterer
> for my mind, and body and fate to match. –
> Oh! The mighty scoundrel! He came and left,
> and said not even his own given name!

(Exit.)

ACT 2

(Enter Feste.)

FESTE
Remember me? Here I am come again!
When no one sees, I slip onto this stage
and run across, just to say these bouncing lines!
I hope you didn't think I'd always rhyme;
That's far too much heady exertion.
But forget everything you've seen, for now
we move our universe to a diff'rent scene.

(Exit Feste.)

SCENE 1

Beach.

Enter Antonio and Sebastian.

ANTONIO
Your health returns in this hot sun, good Sebastian.
No more look'st thou the drowned rat I did pull from sea.
Will you recuperate with me, no longer?

Act 2 Scene 1

SEBASTIAN
By your patience, no. My stars shine darkly o'er
me: the malignancy of my fate might perhaps
distemper yours; therefore shall I crave of you
your leave, that I may bear my evils alone.

ANTONIO
Let me at least know where you are bound.

SEBASTIAN
Where I was bound is no more possible;
I've told you my plans were to sail across the
sea, to the West Indies, and sugar cane.
But the dark and stormy fickle ocean's waves
o'ercame our ship and sunk my plans, and me,
but for thee.
Good friend, let me now tell you more: you
know
my name is Sebastian; my father was that
Sebastian of Messaline, whom I know you
have heard of. He left behind him myself and
a sister, both born in an hour, and
if the heavens had been pleased, would we had
so ended! But you, sir, so altered that;
for some hour before you took me from
the sea, so then was my sister drownèd.

ANTONIO
Alas the day!

SEBASTIAN
A lady, sir, though it was said she much

Act 2 Scene 1

resembled me, was yet of many accounted
beautiful; and she bore a mind that envy
could not but call fair. The sea drowned her, sir,
with salt water, though I seem to drown her
remembrance again with more.

ANTONIO
Good sir, let me help you further.

SEBASTIAN
If you will not undo what you have done, that is,
kill him whom you have recovered, you cannot
help.
Fare ye well at once: my sad state is no fair
company, as I my tears abate.

ANTONIO
But sir, do you even know where you are?

SEBASTIAN
In Illyria, where mine father once was
known, and so to Duke Orsino's court I go.

(Sebastian exits.)

ANTONIO
The gentleness of all the gods go with thee!
I have many enemies in Orsino's court,
else would I go with thee, to cheer thee up from
those darker clouds of stormy sea mem'ries. --
Bah, come what may, good friends are hard to
find;

I'll go with Sebastian into the town, and
hope and trust none there will recall my many
transgressions 'gainst the Duke of years ago.

(He exits.)

SCENE 2

Street.

Enter Viola, with Malvolio following.

MALVOLIO
Hold, hold! Slow your feet!

VIOLA
Does this rude fellow follow me?

MALVOLIO
Were you not even now with the Countess Olivia?

VIOLA
Even now, sir; on a moderate pace I have
since arrived but hither.

MALVOLIO
She returns this ring to you, sir: you might have
saved me my pains, to have taken it away
yourself.

She adds, moreover, that you should put your lord
into a desperate assurance she will none of him,
and requests that you bring word to report
your lord's taking of this.

VIOLA
She took the ring of me: I'll none of it.

MALVOLIO
Come, sir, you peevishly threw it to her.
There it lies, if it be worth stooping for,
if not, be it his that finds it next.

(Malvolio exits.)

VIOLA
I left no ring with her; what means this lady?
Fortune forbid my outside have not charm'd her!
She made good view of me; indeed, so much,
That sure methought her eyes had lost her tongue,
For she did speak in starts distractedly.
She loves me, sure; the cunning of her passion
Invites me in this churlish messenger.
None of my lord's ring! why, he sent her none.
I am the man: if it be so, as 'tis,
Poor lady, she were better love a dream.
How will this fadge? my master loves her dearly;
And I, poor monster, fond as much on him;

And she, mistaken, seems to dote on me.
What thriftless sighs shall poor Olivia breathe!
Oh time! thou must untangle this, not I;
It is too hard a knot for me to untie!

(She exits.)

SCENE 3

Olivia's house, dark at night.

Enter Sir Toby and Sir Andrew with candles and bottles.

SIR TOBY
Approach, Sir Andrew; not to be abed after midnight is to be arise up early.

SIR ANDREW
Nay, my troth, I know not: but I know, to be up late is to be up late.

SIR TOBY
A false conclusion, man. To be up after midnight and to go to bed then, is late, but to be up and stay up through, is early.

SIR ANDREW
Marry, 'tis true.

Act 2 Scene 3

SIR TOBY
And in truth I drink.

SIR ANDREW
But here, we are not alone.

(Enter Feste.)

FESTE
(Aside)
They're drunk, stewed full through.
You got that, right?

SIR TOBY
Welcome, ass. Now, let's have a song.

SIR ANDREW
Thou didst sing so prettily last night for m'lady, troth. I sent thee sixpence for thy hat; didst get it, fool?

FESTE
I did impeticos thy gratillity;
for Malvolio's nose is no whipstock and Myrmidons are no bottle-ale houses.

SIR ANDREW
Excellent! Why, this is the best fooling.

SIR TOBY
Come on; there's sixpence for you: let's have a

song.

FESTE
From you, Sir Toby? But here are two in audience.

SIR ANDREW
Why, here's a sixpence from me, too.

FESTE
Well, then. Wouldst have a love song? or a song of good life?

SIR TOBY
A love song, a love song.

SIR ANDREW
Aye, aye. I care not for good life.

FESTE
(Singing.)
"O mistress mine, where are you roaming?
O, stay and hear; your true love's coming,
That can sing both high and low:
Trip no further, pretty sweeting;
Journeys end in lovers meeting,
Every wise man's son doth know."

SIR ANDREW
Ah, excellent.

Act 2 Scene 3

SIR TOBY

Good, good.

FESTE

(Singing.)

"What is love? 'tis not hereafter;
Present mirth hath present laughter;
What's to come is still unsure:
In delay there lies no plenty;
Then come kiss me, sweet and twenty,
Youth's a stuff will not endure."

SIR ANDREW

A mellifluous voice, as I am true knight.

SIR TOBY

A contagious breath.

SIR ANDREW

Most certain. Shall we?

SIR TOBY

I'll pay you sixpence for your sixpence.

SIR ANDREW

The deal struck, then let's begin.

SIR TOBY

(Singing.)

"Hold thy peace, thou knave"

Act 2 Scene 3

SIR TOBY and SIR ANDREW
(Singing.)
"Thou held me up so brave"

SIR ANDREW
Come, fool, join in.

SIR TOBY and SIR ANDREW
(Singing.)
"I held my peace until I came"

FESTE
(Aside.)
I shall never begin if I hold my piece.

MARIA (O.S.)
Stop that! Cease and desist!

(Enter Maria.)

MARIA
What a caterwauling do you keep here!
If my lady have not called up her steward,
Malvolio, and bid him turn you out of
doors, never trust you me.

SIR TOBY
Oh, fie. Am I not of m'lady's blood?
Am not I consanguineous? Tilly!
(Singing.)
"There dwelt a man in Babylon, lady, lady!"

FESTE
Beshrew me, the knight's in admirable fooling.

SIR TOBY
(Singing.)
"Oh, the twelfth day of December, lady, lady!" –

MARIA
For the love o' God, peace!

(Enter Malvolio.)

MALVOLIO
My masters, are you mad? For shame! Have ye
no wit, manners, nor honesty, but to
gabble like tinkers at this time of night?
Do ye make an alehouse of my lady's house,
that ye squeak out your songs so loudly put?
Is there no respect of place, persons, nor
time in you?

SIR TOBY
We did keep time, sir, in our songs. Quite well,
I think, I myself --

MALVOLIO
Sir Toby, I must be round with you. My lady
bade me tell you, that, though she harbors you
as her kinsman, she's nothing allied to your
disorders. If you can separate yourself and your
misdemeanors, you are welcome to the house; if
not, an it would please you to take leave of her,

she is very willing to bid you farewell.

SIR TOBY
(Singing.)
"Farewell, dear heart, since I must needs be gone."

FESTE
(Singing.)
"His eyes do show his days are almost done."

MALVOLIO
Is't even so?

SIR TOBY
(Singing.)
"But I will never die."

FESTE
Sir Toby, there you lie.

SIR TOBY
Maria, hie there. Another stoup of wine from you, Maria dear!

MALVOLIO
Miss Mary, I see you would give further means for this uncivil rule: my lady shall know of it, by this my witness. For you, it seems, are part of the 'parent problem.

(Malvolio exits.)

Act 2 Scene 3

MARIA
Oh, you! Go shake your ears, you pompous ass.

SIR ANDREW
Must we leave this fine house this night?

SIR TOBY
Malvolio is not my niece, but he
it is she listens to, not me.

MARIA
Sweet Sir Toby, be patient for tonight.
Since the youth of the count's was today with
thy lady, she is much out of quiet.
For Monsieur Malvolio, let me alone
answer him. I fancy I may know a way
to deflate his balloon and out his air.

SIR TOBY
What wilt thou do?

MARIA
I will drop in his way some few obscure
epistles of love; wherein he shall find
himself most feelingly described. I can write
very like my lady your niece.

SIR TOBY
Excellent! I smell a device.

Act 2 Scene 3

FESTE
Oh, Maria, you dev'lish porcupine.

SIR TOBY
He shall think, by the letters that thou wilt drop, that they come from my niece, and that she's in love with him.

MARIA
My purpose is, indeed, a horse of that color.

SIR ANDREW
And your horse now would make him an ass.

MARIA
Ass, I doubt not, for he is already donkey. But for this night, to bed and dream on the event. Farewell.

(She exits.)

SIR TOBY
Come. Come, sir knight; 'tis too late to go to bed now.
Let us begin again:

(They start to leave.)

SIR TOBY and SIR ANDREW
(Singing.)
"Hold thy peace, thou knave;
Thou held me up, so brave!"

(Exit Sir Toby and Sir Andrew.)

FESTE
Aye, me. And to think, 'tis I who's called "Fool!"

(He exits.)

SCENE 4

Duke Orsino's palace.

Enter Duke Orsino, Viola, Curio and others.

DUKE ORSINO
Give me some music. Now, good morrow, friends.
Now, good Cesario, but that piece of song,
that old and antique song we heard last night;
methought it did relieve my passion much,
more than light airs and recollected terms.
Come, but one verse.

CURIO
He is not here, so please your lordship, that should sing it.

DUKE ORSINO
Who was it?

CURIO
Feste, the jester, my lord. A fool that the
lady Olivia's father took much
delight in. He comes about the house, now and
then.

DUKE ORSINO
Seek him out, if he be near, to play the tune
again.

(Exit Curio.)

DUKE ORSINO
Come hither, boy: if ever thou shalt love,
in the sweet pangs of it remember me.

VIOLA
My lord, I shall.

DUKE ORSINO
For such as I am all true lovers are:
afloat betwixt purest joy and total hell.
Hath thine eye yet landed upon thy love, dear
boy?

VIOLA
Aye, yes, my lord, it has, by your favor.

DUKE ORSINO
What kind of woman is't?

Act 2 Scene 4

VIOLA
Of your complexion.

DUKE ORSINO
She is not worth thee, then. What years, i' faith?

VIOLA
About your years, my lord.

DUKE ORSINO
Too old by heaven. Seek thee a younger bride.

(Enter Curio and Feste.)

FESTE
(Aside.)
Look now, I'm over here!
Though here be it the same as there, you know,
as they but move the scenery around.
Didst wonder what caused my absence from m'lady's?
'Tis over here can I pick up some extra coin.

DUKE ORSINO
Oh, fellow, come, the song we had last night.
Mark it, Cesario; it is old and plain.
Come, fool, sing, for twice sixpence more.

FESTE
(Singing.)
"Come away, come away, death,
And in sad cypress let me be laid;

Fly away, fly away breath;
I am slain by a fair cruel maid.
My shroud of white, stuck all with yew,
O, prepare it!
My part of death, no one so true
Did share it.
Not a flower, not a flower sweet
On my black coffin let there be strewn;
Not a friend, not a friend greet
My poor corpse, where my bones shall be
thrown:
A thousand thousand sighs to save,
Lay me, O, where
Sad true lover never find my grave,
To weep there!"

DUKE ORSINO
(Handing him coins.)
There's for thy pains.

FESTE
No pains, sir; I take pleasure in singing, sir.

DUKE ORSINO
I pay thy pleasure, then.

FESTE
Truly, sir, and pleasure will be paid, one time or another.

DUKE ORSINO
Give me now leave to leave thee.

Act 2 Scene 4

FESTE
I leave thee leave to give me leave, my lord.

DUKE ORSINO
Hmm, yes, that's right.

(Feste exits.)

DUKE ORSINO
Let all the rest give place –
Save you, Cesario.

(All else but Cesario exit.)

DUKE ORSINO
Once more, Cesario, I wait no longer;
get thee to yond same sovereign cruelty.
Give her my love, more noble than the world;
impress upon her well, how sick I am.

VIOLA
But if she cannot love you, sir?

DUKE ORSINO
I cannot be so answer'd.

VIOLA
Sooth, but you must.
Say that some lady, as perhaps there is,
hath for your love as great a pang of heart
as you have for Olivia: you cannot love her,

you tell her so; must she not then be answer'd?

DUKE ORSINO
There is no woman could'st love me so much,
as I do love Olivia

VIOLA
Aye, but I know –

DUKE ORSINO
What dost thou know?

VIOLA
Too well what love women to men may owe.
In faith, they are as true of heart as we.
My father had a daughter loved a man,
as it might be, perhaps, were I a woman,
I should your lordship.

DUKE ORSINO
And what's her story?

VIOLA
A blank, my lord. She never told her love,
but let concealment, like a worm i' the bud,
feed on her blushing cheek.

DUKE ORSINO
But died thy sister of her love, boy?

VIOLA
I am all the daughters of my father's house,

and all the brothers, too, and yet I know not.
Sir, shall I to this lady?

DUKE ORSINO
Aye, to her in haste. Give her this jewel; say
my love will brook no more denial.

(Exit.)

SCENE 5

Olivia's garden.

Enter Sir Toby, Sir Andrew and Maria.

MARIA
Quiet thee, now, he's near to hand, I think.
He's been much to himself today, ruminating
on his fortunes, since this morning did I
tell him that m'lady thought him brave and wise.
And the horse's ass accepted such praise
as his due, without suspecting my motive.

SIR TOBY
His head must soon come down a notch.

SIR ANDREW
An we do not, it is pity of our lives.

Act 2 Scene 5

MARIA

Let us all three now into the box tree;
Malvolio's coming down this walk;
he has been yonder in the sun practicing
behavior to his own shadow this half hour.
Observe him, for the love of mockery;
for I know this letter will make a true
contemplative idiot of himself.

> *(She throws down a letter,
> and they withdraw as
> Malvolio enters.)*

MALVOLIO

'Tis but fortune; all is fortune, from top down.
There is example for't; the lady of the Strachy
married the yeoman of her wardrobe.

SIR ANDREW

He's in it, deep.

MARIA

Tush, let not him hear you.

MALVOLIO

Why should'st it not be me, sitting in my robe,
calling my officers to serve my needs,
having just come from a day-bed, where I
have left Olivia sleeping.

SIR TOBY

Fire and brimstone!

Act 2 Scene 5

MARIA
Peace, Sir Toby! Wait till he finds the letter.

MALVOLIO
And then shall I call for my kinsman, Toby, and say, "Cousin Toby, my fortunes having cast me on your niece give me leave to say –

SIR TOBY
What, what?

MALVOLIO
You must amend your drunkenness.

SIR TOBY
Out, scab!

MARIA
Nay, patience, or we break the sinews of our plot.

MALVOLIO
Besides, you waste the treasure of your time with a foolish knight –

SIR ANDREW
That's me, I warrant you.

MALVOLIO
One Sir Andrew –

SIR ANDREW
I knew 'twas I, for many call me fool.

MALVOLIO
But what employment do we have here?

(He takes up the letter and begins to read.)

MARIA
Yes, the woodcock's got it!

SIR TOBY
Didst thou copy m'lady's hand well, vixen?

MARIA
Well 'nuff, I warrant, for Malvolio's eyes.

MALVOLIO
By my life, this is my lady's hand – these be her very C's, her U's and her T's.

MARIA
Told you!

MALVOLIO
(Reading.)
"To the unknown beloved, this, and my good wishes" – her very phrases! By your leave, 'tis her wax. And 'tis her seal, pressed true: 'tis from my lady, but to whom?

Act 2 Scene 5

SIR TOBY
This wins him, liver and all.

MALVOLIO
(Reading.)
"Jove knows, I love. No man must know.
I may command where I adore.
M, O, my man, doth sway my life."

SIR ANDREW
Is that a riddle?

SIR TOBY
Well, done, girl. That's got him.

MALVOLIO
M – O --
M – M – why that begins my name, Malvolio.
And O, well O is the letter ends my name!
"I may command where I adore" Why, she may command me: I serve her, she is my lady.

MARIA
There's yet more, should the fool read on.

MALVOLIO
M, O, M, O – it must mean me. There follows prose:
"Be not afraid of greatness: some
are born great, some achieve greatness, and
some have greatness thrust upon 'em. Thy Fates
open their hands; let thy blood and spirit

embrace them. Be more a man. Be
opposite with a kinsman, surly with servants; let
thy tongue tang arguments of state; she thus
advises thee that sighs for thee. Remember who
commended thy yellow stockings, and wished to
see thee ever cross-gartered: I say, remember."
Oh, my stars! I have worn such yellow
stockings!
I do not now fool myself, to let imagination jade
me; for every reason excites to this, that my lady
loves me. She did commend my yellow
stockings of late, she did praise my leg being
cross-gartered;
and in this she manifests herself to my love, and
with a kind of injunction drives me to these
habits of her liking. –
I will be proud, I will read politic authors,
I will baffle Sir Toby and all servants. Jove and
my stars be praised! Here is yet a
postscript.
(Reading.)
"Thou canst not show you know my love. Let it
appear in thy smiling; thy smiles become thee
well; therefore in my presence still smile, dear
my sweet, I prithee."
And then 'tis sealed with a bright red kiss.
Jove, I thank thee: I will smile; I will do
everything that she wilt now have of me.

(He exits.)

SIR TOBY
I could marry this wench for this device.

SIR ANDREW
So could I too.

MARIA
Come, gents, let us down from tree.

(They come forth.)

SIR TOBY
What say, wench? Wilst have me? I ask of thee no other dowry, but that you dream up such another jest.

MARIA
Peace, lord, lest I begin to take you at your word. If you will then see the fruits of the sport, mark his first approach before my lady: he will come to her in yellow stockings and 'tis a color she abhors, and cross-gartered, a fashion she detests. If you will see it, follow me.

SIR TOBY
To the gates of Tartar, thou most excellent devil of wit!

(They exit.)

ACT 3

Enter Feste with a small drum.

FESTE
I have a drum! I have drum! Hear me roar!
(He beats upon the drum.)
This be music, gentles, feel free to love!
Sixpence, tuppence even, or more perchance,
for some of you out there I see in such fine pants,
with bulging – uh – wallets, and ladies wearing
such fine jewels! Thou most clearly can afford a
shilling or three for little me!
What, none? Oh misers and frosty snowmen you be,
to let me play and starve for thee.
[*if a coin is tossed onstage:*
Oh, happy day! a coin, maybe another?
Maybe? I'm rich, marry, and soon can me retire
to a lakeside cabin, and smoke silly stuff
all day, with the rest of you pillow sitters!]
Oops, but I near forget, my place is needed.
(He rushes to his mark.)
Hush now – no, really hold your applause.
'Tis embarrassing me, stop now. [Thanks, mom.]
Shhhhhhhhhhhhhhhhhhhhhhhhhhhhhh.
I trust you all remember, the play continues.
Marry, the show must go on.

SCENE 1

Olivia's garden.

Enter Viola.

VIOLA
Save thee, friend, and thy music. Dost thou live by thy drum?

FESTE
No, ma'am – oops, I mean, sir. I live by the church.

VIOLA
Art thou a churchman?

FESTE
Not at all, I just live near by.

VIOLA
Art thou Lady Olivia's fool?

FESTE
No, indeed …sir. The Lady Olivia has no folly; she will keep no fool … sir, till she's married. And fools are as like husbands as herrings are to swordfish; the husband's the bigger. I am indeed not her fool, but her corrupter of words.

VIOLA
I saw thee late at the Count Orsino's.

FESTE
Foolery …sir, does walk about the orb like
the sun, it shines everywhere. I gladly play
at both households, corrupting fair evenly.

VIOLA
Corrupt me no more, dark as I am become.
Hold, there's expenses for thee.

(She tosses him a coin.)

FESTE
Now, by Jove, blessings be! If only he
would send thee a manly beard.

VIOLA
By my troth, I'll tell thee, I am almost sick for
one. Is thy lady within?

FESTE
hmmmm … would not a pair of these have bred,
sir?

VIOLA
Yes, being kept together and put to use.

FESTE
I would corrupt thee less, and sing you more,

to bring a mate to this lone soldier.

VIOLA
I understand you, sir; 'tis well begged.

(She tosses him a second coin.)

FESTE
The offense, I hope, is not great ... sir, begging
that is. My lady is within, sir. I will
construe to them whence you came, if not who
you are.

(Feste exits.)

VIOLA
This fellow is wise enough to play the fool;
and to do that well craves a kind of wit.
I must remember me well not to forget,
lest I on the bad side on yon fool regret.

(Enter Sir Toby and Sir Andrew.)

SIR TOBY
Save you, gentleman.

VIOLA
And to you two gentlemen, too.

Act 3 Scene 1

SIR TOBY
Will you encounter the house? My niece is
desirous you should enter, if you come for her.

VIOLA
She is indeed the target of my aim.

(Enter Olivia and Maria.)

OLIVIA
You needn't pull too hard upon your bow,
thy target, good young sir, has come to you.

SIR ANDREW
Speak you now, boy; let's hear Orsino's words.

VIOLA
My matter hath no voice, to your own most
pregnant and vouchsafed ear.

OLIVIA
Let the garden door be shut, and leave me to my
hearing.

*(Exit Sir Toby, Sir Andrew
and Maria.)*

OLIVIA
Give me your hand, sir.

VIOLA
My duty, madam, and most humble service.

Act 3 Scene 1

OLIVIA
What is your name?

VIOLA
Cesario is your servant's name, fair princess.

OLIVIA
My servant, sir! 'Twas never merry world
since lowly feigning was called compliment:
You are servant to the Count Orsino, youth.

VIOLA
And he is yours, and his needs be yours:
your servant's servant is your servant, madam.

OLIVIA
Were he my servant, I would command him
think not on me. You're servant of his servant;
let you be also his heart of his heart.

VIOLA
Madam -- I come to whet your gentle thoughts
on his behalf.

OLIVIA
Oh, by your leave, I pray you,
I bade you never speak again of him;
but, would you undertake another suit,
I had rather hear you to solicit that
than music from the spheres.

Act 3 Scene 1

VIOLA
Dear lady –

OLIVIA
Give me leave, beseech you. I did send,
after the last enchantment you did here,
a ring in chase of you. My pardons, sir,
for clumsy that was. So did I abuse you.
Under your hard construction must I sit,
to force that on you, in a shameful cunning,
which you knew none of yours: what might you think?
Have you not set my honor back at the stake
and baited it with all the unmuzzled thoughts
that lusty heart can think? I wear no more veil
before you, sir; I'm bare. My soul is here.
Thirsty. And hungry.
Let me hear you speak.

VIOLA
I pity you.

OLIVIA
What, pity? That's a degree of love.

VIOLA
In this instance, no. I cannot, dear lady.

OLIVIA
Then there lies your way, due west.

Act 3 Scene 1

VIOLA

Then westward-ho! Grace and good disposition
attend your ladyship. You'll nothing, madam,
to my lord by me?

OLIVIA

Stay –
I prithee, tell me what thou thinkest of me.

VIOLA

That you do think you are not what you are.

OLIVIA

If I think so, I think the same of you.

VIOLA

Then think you right. I am not what I am.

OLIVIA

I would you were as I would have you be!

VIOLA

Would it be better, madam, than I am?
I wish I might, for now I am your fool.

OLIVIA

Cesario, by the roses of the spring,
by maidhood, honor, truth and everything,
I love thee so, that naught can my passion hide.
Do not extort thy reasons from this clause,
for that I woo, thou therefore hast no cause,
but rather reason thus with my unfetter'd lips.

(She kisses Viola.)

VIOLA
By innocence I swear, and by my youth,
what have I here is for no woman's touch.
And so adieu, good madam; never more
will I my master's tears to you deplore.

OLIVIA
Yet come again, for thou perhaps mayst move
thy heart, which now abhors, to like his love.

(They exit.)

SCENE 2

Olivia's house.

Enter Sir Toby and Sir Andrew.

SIR ANDREW
No, 'swounds. I'll not stay a jot longer.

SIR TOBY
But why, good knight?

SIR ANDREW
Marry, I saw your niece do more favors to

the count's serving man than ever she bestowed
upon me. I saw't in the orchard.

SIR TOBY
Did she see thee the while, old boy? tell me that.

SIR ANDREW
As plain as I see you now.

SIR TOBY
Then there's to that, good proof you should stay
to woo.
She did show favor to the youth in your sight
only to exasperate you, to awake
your dormouse valor, to put fire in your woo.
You should then have accosted her, and with
some excellent jests, fire-new from the mint, you
should have banged the youth into dumbness.
Alack, you've now sailed into the north of my
lady's opinion, where you hang like an
icicle on a Dutchman's beard, unless you
redeem it by some laudable attempt
either of valor or of policy.

SIR ANDREW
I'm not much good as a politician.

SIR TOBY
Why, then, build me your fortunes upon the
basis of valor. Challenge the upstart youth,
to fight with him; my niece will take note of it.
There is no love-broker in the whole world

can more prevail in man's commendation
with woman than report of that man's valor.

SIR ANDREW
By heavens, yes! Will you challenge him to me?

SIR TOBY
Go, write it in a martial hand; be curst and brief;
it is no matter how witty thou tweaks.
Taunt him with license of paper and ink.
Let there be gall enough in thy ink, though thou
write with a goose pen, no matter. About it.

SIR ANDREW
I will!

(Sir Andrew exits, as Maria enters.)

MARIA
Good, Sir Toby, how is it with you non?

SIR TOBY
The better, having you grace my presence.

MARIA
If you desire the spleen, and will laugh yourself
into stitches, follow me. Yond gull Malvolio is
in yellow stockings.

SIR TOBY
And cross gartered?

Act 3 Scene 2

MARIA
Most villainously. He does obey every
point of the letter that I dropped to betray him.
I can hardly forbear hurling things at him;
I know my lady will strike him. If she do,
he'll smile and take't for a great favor.

SIR TOBY
Come, bring us, bring us where he is.

(Exit.)

SCENE 3

Street.

Enter Sebastian and Antonio.

SEBASTIAN
Though I sought not to trouble you, still are
thou well met, for none here do I know well.

ANTONIO
I could not stay behind you: my desire
for adventure did spur me forth.

SEBASTIAN
My kind Antonio,
I can no other answer make but thanks,

and thanks; and ever more, thanks to your help.
Now here, in Orsino's town, what's to do?
Shall we go see the sights?

ANTONIO
Tomorrow, sir; best first go see to your lodging.

SEBASTIAN
I am not weary, and 'tis long to night;
I pray you, let us satisfy our eyes
with what's to see that does renown this city.

ANTONIO
Good sir … but would you pardon me?
I do not without danger walk these streets.
Once, in a sea-fight, 'gainst the County's galleys
I did some service, of such note indeed
that were I taken here it would mean my life.

SEBASTIAN
Belike you slew great number of his people.

ANTONIO
The offense was not of such a bloody nature;
more like a sudden infiltration and then
the loss of precious gold from chests within, and
much noise and general clamor from others,
while I alone in scarlet pantaloons
did in sunset light stand out upon the deck,
and I fear my face wouldst now well be known.

Act 3 Scene 3

SEBASTIAN
Do not then walk too open.

ANTONIO
It doth not fit me. Here, sir, here's my purse.
Some streets yet that way, at the Elephant,
is best to lodge. I will meet thee there.

SEBASTIAN
Why I your purse?

ANTONIO
Haply, your eye may light upon some toy
you have desire to purchase.

SEBASTIAN
With thanks, again, I'll leave you for an hour.

ANTONIO
To the Elephant.

SEBASTIAN
I do remember.

SCENE 4

Olivia's garden.

Enter Olivia and Maria.

OLIVIA
I have sent after him; he says he'll come.
Oh, Maria, is not this youth divine?
How shall I feast him? What bestow of him?
I must make preparations. –
Where is Malvolio? 'Tis not time to slack.
I should benefit from his calm demeanor.

MARIA
He's coming, madam; but in a very strange
manner. He is, today, possessed, madam.

OLIVIA
Why, what's the matter? Is he sick?

MARIA
No, madam, he does nothing but smile: your
ladyship were best to have some guard about
you, for, sure, the man is tainted in's wits.

OLIVIA
Go call him hither.

(Exit Maria.)

Act 3 Scene 4

OLIVIA
I am mad myself,
if sad and merry madness equal be.

(Enter Maria with Malvolio.)

MALVOLIO
Sweet lady, ho, ho.

OLIVIA
Smilest thou?
I sent for thee upon a sad occasion.

MALVOLIO
Sad, lady! I could be sad: this doth make some obstruction in the blood, this cross-gartering. But what of that? If it please the eye of one, it is with me as if was golden butter on rye.

OLIVIA
Why, how dost thou, man? What is the matter with thee?

MALVOLIO
Not black in my mind, though yellow in my legs.

OLIVIA
Malvolio, I fear thee may be ill.
Wilt thou go to bed, Malvolio?

Act 3 Scene 4

MALVOLIO
To bed! Aye, sweetheart, and I'll come with thee.

OLIVIA
God comfort thee! Why dost thy smile and stretch thy leg toward me?

MARIA
How, now? Why appear you so bold, Malvolio?

MALVOLIO
"Be not afraid of greatness" – was well writ.

OLIVIA
What meanest thou by that, Malvolio?

MALVOLIO
"Some are born great" --

OLIVIA
What?

MALVOLIO
"And some have greatness thrust upon them."

OLIVIA
Heaven restore thee!

MALVOLIO
"Remember who commended thy yellow stockings."

OLIVIA
Why, this is midsummer madness.

(Enter Sir Toby.)

SIR TOBY
Sweet niece, the young gentleman of the Count
Orsino's is returned. I could hardly
entreat him back. He waits upon the gates.

OLIVIA
I'll come to him.
Dear uncle Toby, this man, Malvolio,
seems besotted today, perhaps in your
field of expertise and care. Do watch him, sir.

(Exit Olivia and Maria.)

MALVOLIO
(Aside.)
Oh, ho! Do you come near me now? No worse
man than Sir Toby to look to me! This
concurs directly with the letter: she
sends him on purpose, that I may appear
stubborn to him; for she incites to that
in the letter. I am on track to her love!

SIR TOBY
How is't with you, sir?

MALVOLIO
Go off; I discard you. Let me enjoy my privates.

SIR TOBY
Your privates, sir, seem too tightly abound
for you to seek any true enjoyment.

MALVOLIO
Be gone, you couthless cad!

(Enter Maria.)

MARIA
(Aside.)
Lo, how hollow the fiend speaks with him!

SIR TOBY
He seems mad, no doubt ill of a sudden.

MALVOLIO
Do you know what you say?

SIR TOBY
I have some experience with mental
cases of distraction in the Far East.
'Tis best we be gentle –
How do you do, Malvolio?

MARIA
Pray God, he be not bewitched!

MALVOLIO
Bewitched? How now, mistress!

Act 3 Scene 4

MARIA
Oh, Lord! He's dangerous!

SIR TOBY
Prithee, hold thy peace, Malvolio.
How now, my bawcock! How dost thou, chuck?

MALVOLIO
Sir!

SIR TOBY
Aye, biddy, come with me. Let's put you down to sleep, perhaps with soft restraints upon thy arms.

MARIA
Get him to say his prayers, good Sir Toby; get him to pray.

MALVOLIO
My prayers, minx!

MARIA
No, it seems he will not hear of godliness.

MALVOLIO
Go, hang yourselves all! You are idle shallow things. I am not of your element; you shall know more hereafter.

(He exits.)

SIR TOBY
You are a genius.

MARIA
Nay, pursue him now, lest the device take air and taint.

SIR TOBY
Come, we'll have him in a dark room and bound.
My niece is already in the belief that he's mad. We may carry it thus, for our pleasure and his penance.

(Enter Sir Andrew.)

SIR ANDREW
Here's the challenge, writ out with vinegar and pepper in't.

SIR TOBY
'Tis saucy?

MARIA
What's this?

SIR ANDREW
I warrant it shall do.

(He hands the letter to Sir Toby.)

Act 3 Scene 4

SIR TOBY
(Reading.)
"Thou comest hard upon the good Lady
Olivia, who in my sight uses thee
kindly; but thou liest in thy youthful throat."
Well, so far; brief but coming, I see, to a climax.

SIR ANDREW
I took first in letters in my class.

SIR TOBY
(Reading.)
"I will waylay thee going home, where if it
be thy chance to kill me" –

MARIA
Oh, this cannot end well.

SIR TOBY
(Reading.)
"Thou killest me like a rogue and a villain.
Fare thee well, and God have mercy upon
one of our souls. He may have mercy upon
mine; but my hope is better, and so look to
thyself. Thy friend, as thou usest him, and thy
sworn enemy, Andrew Aguecheek."
Go, Sir Andrew, look for him in the orchard.
I will present your challenge. He is even
now with my niece, and God knows what they do,
even as we speak.

Act 3 Scene 4

SIR ANDREW
Make haste, Sir Toby, for surely there is cause
for thee as kin and me as knight to fear
my lady's repute and honor be at risk.

(Sir Andrew exits.)

MARIA
You work a device of your own, I see, and
fairly brilliant it is, too.

SIR TOBY
Now will I not deliver this letter. For
this letter, being so excellently
ignorant, will breed no terror in the youth;
he will find it comes from a clodpole. Instead,
I will deliver his challenge by word of
mouth; set upon Aguecheek a notable
report of valor, and drive the gentleman,
as full of vim as young men are, into a
most hideous state of rage and fury.
This will so fright them both that they will kill
one another by the look, like cockroaches.

MARIA
Wilt that not hurt thy friend?

SIR TOBY
'Tis just fun and games, fine maiden. Thou hast
seen the youth and Aguecheek: neither could
brandish a sword to hurt a flea.
Fetch me a topped-off flagon, for brain's power.

Act 3 Scene 4

I will meditate upon some horrid
message for a challenge.

(Enter Olivia and Viola.

*Exit Maria, while Sir Toby
withdraws.)*

OLIVIA
Here, wear this jewel for me; 'tis my picture;
refuse it not; it hath no tongue to vex you;
and I beseech you come again tomorrow.
What shall you ask of me that I'll deny?

VIOLA
Nothing but this: your true love for my master.

OLIVIA
How may I give him what I have given you?

VIOLA
I will release you, madam.

OLIVIA
Well, come again tomorrow. Fare thee well.

*(Olivia exits, and Sir Toby
comes forward.)*

SIR TOBY
Gentleman, God save thee.

VIOLA
And you, sir.

SIR TOBY
What defense thou hast, betake thee to it. I
know not what wrongs thou hast done him, but I
know thy challenger: a knight full of despite,
bloody as the hunter, steadfast as the hangman;
he who hast proven himself in foreign wars,
to be a right fistful of fury when wronged.
He attends thee at the orchard-end.

VIOLA
You mistake, sir; I am sure no man hath any
quarrel to me.

SIR TOBY
You'll find it otherwise, I assure you; beware,
for your man awaits, upon thy honor.

VIOLA
I pray you, sir, what is he?

SIR TOBY
He is a knight, and a devil in private
brawl. Souls and bodies hath he divorced thrice.

VIOLA
I will return again into the house and desire
some conduct of the lady. I am no fighter. I have
heard of some kind of men that put quarrels
purposely on others, to taste their valor. Belike

SIR TOBY
Sir, no. His indignation derives itself out of a
very competent injury; therefore, get you on and
give him his desire. Back you shall not to the
house.

VIOLA
This is as uncivil as strange. I beseech you, do
me this courteous office, as to ask of the knight
what my offense to him may be?

SIR TOBY
I will do so. Walk you that way, there, and I
shall return with your answer, soon.

(Sir Toby exits.)

VIOLA
This is so much strange, stranger even than
that man chasing me down with the lady's ring.
If this be another of her machinations,
I fail to see how love for her would come from
forcing me to duel. What a land of cuckoos!

(Exit Viola.

Enter Sir Toby and Sir Andrew.)

SIR TOBY

Why, man, he's a devil; I have not seen such
vinegar. They say he has taught fencing,
in Paris.

SIR ANDREW

Pox on't, then, man. I'll not meddle with him.

SIR TOBY

Aye, but he will not now be pacified. I
could hardly get ahead of him, to warn you.

SIR ANDREW

Plague on't! An I'd known he had been so
cunning in the foil, and rapier too, no doubt, I'd
never have issued challenge. Let him let
the matter slip, and I'll give him my horse, Chip.

SIR TOBY

I'll make the motion. Stand here, make a good
show on't. Look thou fierce, and perchance this
shall end without the perdition of your soul.

(Enter Viola.)

SIR TOBY
(To Viola.)

There's no remedy, sir; he will fight with you.
Marry, he finds that now there is scarce worth
talking of; therefore, draw, for the supportance
of his vow. He protests he will but make a show,
and will not hurt you, much.

VIOLA
(Aside.)
Pray God defend me, this sword is for show
as just needful part of my man's disguise;
I know not how to use it, nor why I should.

SIR TOBY
(To Sir Andrew.)
Come, Sir Andrew, there's no remedy; the
gentleman will, for his honor's sake, have
but one bout with you. He has promised me, he
will not hurt you, much.

SIR ANDREW
I am here.

VIOLA
I do assure you, 'tis against my will.

(Enter Antonio.)

ANTONIO
Put up your sword. If this young gentleman
have done offence, I take the fault on me.
If you offend him, I for him defy you.

SIR TOBY
What, now? You, sir! Why, what are you?

ANTONIO
A friend of this encaptured youth's, dear sir,

and not one to back away from a fight.

SIR ANDREW
But sir –

ANTONIO
Draw!

(They draw.)

SIR TOBY
Sir Andrew, if ever thou wert a knight!

(Enter Officers.)

FIRST OFFICER
Hold! This here, this is the man. Do thy office.

SECOND OFFICER
Antonio, I arrest thee at the suit of Count Orsino.

ANTONIO
You do mistake me, officers.

FIRST OFFICER
No, sir, no jot; I know your favor well,
though now you have no sea-cap on your head.
Take him away: he knows I know him well.

ANTONIO
I must obey.
(To Viola.)

This comes from seeking you. Have you spent my purse in whole, upon your new dandy clothes?

VIOLA
Sir?

SECOND OFFICER
Come, Antonio.

ANTONIO
Anon, anon.
(To Viola.)
I must entreat of you some of that money.

VIOLA
What money, sir?
For the kindness you have showed me here, I'll lend you something. I haven't much, but here's half of what little coin I have with me.

SECOND OFFICR
Come, sir, I pray you go.

ANTONIO
Let me speak a little. This youth that you see here I snatch'd one half out of the jaws of death.

FIRST OFFICER
What's that to us? The time goes by, all day.

Act 3 Scene 4

ANTONIO
Oh! But how vile an idol proves this god!
Thou hast, Sebastian, done thy good features
shame.

FIRST OFFICER
We go!

SECOND OFFICER
Away with you, Antonio.

(Exit Antonio and the Officers.)

VIOLA
He called me Sebastian!

SIR TOBY
(To Sir Andrew.)
Come hither, knight. See how the fellow withers.
I think he's not nearly so ferocious.
Let us escape this witch's brew and find for
ourselves a mead of more satisfying quench.

(Exit Sir Toby and Sir Andrew.)

VIOLA
He named Sebastian. My brother whom I see
now only whenst I look in my glass, for
even so in this favor was my brother,
and him it is I imitate. Yet how does

this Antonio know the name?

(Exit.)

ACT 4

Enter Feste.

FESTE
Whew! Oh, me, oh! My heart still palpitates, for
fear for sweet Viola nee Cesario!
Who here thought she a goner?
You? You? I saw you shiver, I did.
You no doubt noticed I was not much in that
last whole act, and were I paid by per my word
starve I would upon this stage!
Come gentles, do not forget your applause
for dear old Feste, jester to kings and queens,
but remember you, too, that I like silver!

SCENE 1

Before Olivia's house.

Enter Sebastian.

FESTE
Ah, how are you, dear ... sir?

SEBASTIAN
I'm sorry. Do I know you?

Act 4 Scene 1

FESTE
Will you make believe that I am not sent for
you by her, m'lady Olivia, your consort?

SEBASTIAN
Go to, go to, thou art a foolish fellow:
let me be clear of thee.

FESTE
Well held out, i' faith! No, I do not know you;
nor I am not sent to you by my lady, to bid you
come speak with her; nor your name is not
Cesario; nor this is not my nose neither. Nothing
that is so is so.

SEBASTIAN
I prithee, vent thy folly somewhere else; thou
know'st not me.

FESTE
Vent my folly! He has heard that word of some
great man and now applies it to a fool. Vent
my folly! I am afraid to vent, of my
own. Ungird thy strangeness and tell me what I
shall vent to my lady: shall I vent to her
that thou art coming?

SEBASTIAN
I prithee, foolish clown, depart from me. There's
money for thee. Be gone.

FESTE
(Aside.)
See how he does pay the fool for being fool!
It's not too late for any of you out there;
what say? What say? Are any coins coming my
way? Silver? Eh?

(Enter Sir Andrew and Sir Toby.)

SIR ANDREW
Now, sir, have I met you again? There's for you.

(Sir Andrew slaps Sebastian.)

SEBASTIAN
Why, there's for thee!

(He slaps Sir Andrew.)

SIR TOBY
But hold, young gentleman. How dare you attack?

(Sir Toby slaps Sebastian.)

SEBASTIAN
And there's for thee!

(He slaps Sir Toby.)

Act 4 Scene 1

SEBASTIAN
Are all you people mad?

FESTE
(Turning back to the action.)
But what's this sudden animosity?

SIR TOBY
Good sir, you have affronted us both and must
now feel the steel of these two knights, together.

SEBASTIAN
Though thou number two, still will I meet you!

(They draw and fight.)

FESTE
This will I tell my lady straight: she will these
blades sheath harmlessly and restore the peace.

(Feste exits.)

SIR TOBY
Good sir, against two shalt thou tire quickly;
already I admit I am feeling spent;
surely you must it feel doubly so, eh?

SEBASTIAN
I'm just warming up, old man!

SIR ANDREW
Perhaps we could settle on a game of cards?

Act 4 Scene 1

SEBASTIAN
Oh, mad fellows, why then did you challenge me?

SIR TOBY
In troth, I remember not! Sir Andrew?

SIR ANDREW
Nor I! I'm certain 'twas something to o'erlook.

(Enter Olivia.)

OLIVIA
Sir Toby! On thy life I charge thee, hold!

(They cease fighting.)

SIR TOBY
Madam!

OLIVIA
Will it be ever thus? Ungracious wretches,
fit for the mountains and the barbarous caves,
where manners ne'er were preached! Out of my sight!
Be not offended, dear Cesario. Come.

(Exit Sir Toby and Sir Andrew.)

OLIVIA
I prithee, gentle friend,
Come with me, come in with me to my house,
and hear thou there how many fruitless pranks
this ruffian hath botch'd up, that thou thereby
may smile at this.

SEBASTIAN
What relish is this? How runs the stream?
An I am mad, or else this is a dream:
if it be thus to dream, still let me sleep!

(They exit, Olivia pulling him inside.)

SCENE 2

Enter Maria and Feste.

MARIA
Nay, I prithee, put on this gown and this beard;
make believe thou art Sir Mompas the curate: do
it quickly: I'll call Sir Toby the whilst.

(Maria exits.)

FESTE
Well, I'll put it on, and I will dissemble myself
in't, to play this game the way she wishes.
'Tis a madhouse, sure, what with knighted fools

a-chasing each other out of doors, and here
inside I find poor Malvolio locked up
for nothing more than fun and games on him.

(Enter Sir Toby and Maria.)

SIR TOBY
Jove bless thee, father Mompas.

FESTE
Bonos dies, Sir Toby; for sixpence I am
your man and wilt be this Father Mompas as
need be, willy nilly; where do I go?

SIR TOBY
To him, Sir Mompas.

(He guides Feste to Malvolio's cell.)

FESTE
What, ho, I say! Peace in this prison!

MALVOLIO (O.S.)
Who calls there?

FESTE
Sir Mompas the curate, who comes to visit
Malvolio the lunatic.

(Malvolio comes to the door.)

Act 4 Scene 2

MALVOLIO
Sir Mompas, Sir Mompas, good Sir Mompas, go to my lady.

FESTE
Out , hyperbolical fiend! How vex't thou this man!
Talkest thou nothing but of ladies?

SIR TOBY
Well said, Master Mompas.

MALVOLIO
Sir Mompas, never was man thus wronged: good Sir Mompas, do not think I am mad: they have laid me here in hideous darkness.

FESTE
Fie, thou dishonest Satan! I call thee by the most modest terms; for I am one of those gentle ones that will use the devil himself with courtesy. Sayest thou that house is dark?

MALVOLIO
As hell, Sir Mompas.

FESTE
Why it hath bay windows as barricadoes, and the clearstores toward the south north are as lustrous as ebony, and yet complainest thou of obstruction?

Act 4 Scene 2

MALVOLIO
I am not mad, Sir Mompas. I say to you, this house is dark.

FESTE
Madman, thou errst: I say, there is no darkness but ignorance; in which thou art more puzzled than the Egyptians in their fog.

MALVOLIO
I say this house is dark as ignorance; and was never a man so abused! I am no more mad than you; make trial of it in any question, Sir Mompas!

FESTE
What is the opinion of Pythagoras concerning wild fowl?

MALVOLIO
What?

FESTE
Would fourteen men love thirteen women?

MALVOLIO
Are these riddles? What want you of me, Sir Mompas?

FESTE
Good lunatic, these are but standard questions of diagnosis; shall we proceed?

MALVOLIO
But make sense, good sir!

FESTE
Cuckoo.

MALVOLIO
What?

FESTE
Oh, dear, thine status is too far gone, belike.
Dost thou still find it dark?

MALVOLIO
It is dark in here!

FESTE
Oh, dear, oh, dear. Fare thee well, simple lunatic.
Remain thee there in self-imposed darkness.

(Feste, Sir Toby and Maria withdraw.)

SIR TOBY
Here is your sixpence, master prevaricator.

FESTE
And some say I am the fool.

MARIA
King of fools, of certainty.

FESTE
Why, thankee, madam.

SIR TOBY
Now back to sound him, using thine own voice,
and bring me word of how thou findest him.
I would be done, for I am so far in
offense with my niece that I cannot pursue
with any safety this sport to its upshot.
Come by and by to my chamber.

(Feste accepts another coin, and Sir Toby and Maria exit.)

FESTE
(Coming forth, singing.)
"Hey, Robin, jolly Robin.
Tell me how thy lady does.
My lady is unkind, perdy." --

MALVOLIO
Fool, fool!

FESTE
Ack, who speaks? Who calls?

MALVOLIO
Fool, 'tis Malvolio, over here.

FESTE
Master Malvolio?

Act 4 Scene 2

MALVOLIO
Aye, fool; bring me a candle, and paper
and ink; as I am a gentleman, I
will thank thee for't.

FESTE
Alas, sir, how fell you into darkness?

MALVOLIO
Yes, it is darkness, indeed, yes!

FESTE
Yes, of course. Are you well, sir?

MALVOLIO
They have propertied me here; keep me in
darkness, send ministers to me to cause me to
doubt my sanity.

FESTE
Yes, the minister is still here. Good sir!
(Stepping out of Malvolio's view, and using the voice of Sir Mompas.)
Ahem, yes, fool? Why aggravate you this
lunatic?
(In his own voice.)
But learnèd sir, is he really lunatic?
(Using the voice of Sir Mompas.)
Ad philly circumstitus, of certainty, more the

shame, and yet less humbicumilitus.
>(In his own voice.)
Oh, God, of course, how terribly so sad.
Do you go now, sir?
>(As Sir Mompas.)
I have a cave to visit, where sits a
hermit of several years, so fare thee well,
wise fool.

>(Stepping back in front of
>Malvolio again.)

FESTE
Oh, yes, fare thee well, oh mysterious one.
Malvolio, I just spoke with the learnèd
minister!

MALVOLIO
Yes, I heard, fool, you were but two feet away.
You would have to believe me fool, to think I
did not hear you clear.

FESTE
Oh, no, sir, not at all, thou art mad, not fool.
An if thee heard, then heard you him call me a
"wise fool", is't not so?

MALVOLIO
Bring me, wise fool, some ink, paper and light,
and convey what I will set down to my lady,
then shall I call you whatever more thee like.

Act 4 Scene 2

FESTE
Have you any money, sir?

MALVOLIO
Fool, I'm locked up with nothing here, but dark.

FESTE
(Singing.)

"I am gone, sir,
And anon, sir,
I'll be with you again,
In a trice,
Like to the old Vice,
Your need to sustain;
Who, with dagger of lath,
In his rage and his wrath,
Cries, ah, ha! to the devil:
Like a mad lad,
Pare thy nails, dad;
Adieu, good man devil."
Adieu, lunatic, adieu.

MALVOLIO
Fool!

(Feste exits and Malvolio withdraws.)

SCENE 3

Olivia's garden.

Enter Sebastian.

SEBASTIAN
This air, this garden, this glorious sun!
This pearl she gave me, I've never seen its like.
Is all this madness? Where's Antonio, then?
I could not find him at the Elephant.
I would he came here to share in this bounty!
Yet doth this accident and flood of fortune
so far exceed all instance, all discourse,
that I am ready to distrust mine eyes
and wrangle with my reason that persuades me
to any other trust but that I am mad
or else the lady's mad; yet, if 'twere so,
she could not sway her house, command her followers,
take and give back affairs and their dispatch
with such a smooth, discreet and stable bearing
as I perceive she does.

(Enter Olivia.)

OLIVIA
Blame not this haste of mine. If you mean well,
now to church with me, under consecrated roof,
plight me the full assurance of your faith.
That my most jealous and too doubtful soul

Act 4 Scene 3

may live at peace. What do you say?

SEBASTIAN
I'll pledge my being and my soul to you;
and, having sworn truth, ever will be true.

OLIVIA
Come, saucy boy, and make a woman of
thy love.

(Exit.)

ACT 5

Enter Feste.

FESTE
Act 5, my friends and company, act 5!
We've come so far, and have but bits of time left
in which to confiscate and celebrate
our happiness, good cheer and merry wallets.
No! No, good sir, no fine madam, take not your
coins out from your tight pockets to throw at
me. Not yet. --
Do it not, I say, for you've held your reward
so long, wait now till we up here all are done
and you can then heap mountains of earn'd praise
upon our heads, by standing on your feet,
hooting, hollering and pure walloping, and
clapping as wildly as you e'er did before
for any comedy.
But first – we must see how this doth finish.
Will there be bloody duel or blushing bride?
Let's see, shall we?

SCENE 1

Before Olivia's house.

Enter Duke Orsino, Viola, Curio and Lords.

FESTE
Good sir, is this a party that you take
to the house of my lady, Countess Olivia?

DUKE ORSINO
Marry, fool, I am done sending messengers.
I've come myself, and will suffer no delay.
If you will let your lady know I
am here to speak with her, and bring her back
here with you, I've a purse of ducats for thee.

FESTE
Ducats?
            (Aside.)
That's like dollars!
            (To the Duke.)
Marry, sir, lullaby to your bounty till I come
again. I go sir. Toot toot!

(He exits.)

Act 5 Scene 1

VIOLA
Here comes the man, sir, that did rescue me.

(Enter Antonio and Officers.)

DUKE ORSINO
That face of his I remember well;
yet, when I saw it last, it was besmear'd
as black as Vulcan in the smoke of war.
A bawbling vessel was he captain of,
with which he took our finest sea vessel
and ransacked her stores most valuable.

FIRST OFFICER
Orsino, this is Antonio
that took the Phoenix and stripped her royals bare.
Here in the streets, desperate of shame and state,
in private battle did we apprehend him.

VIOLA
He did me kindness, sir, drew on my side;
but in conclusion put strange speech upon me.

DUKE ORSINO
Notable pirate! Thou salt-water thief!
What foolish boldness brought thee to their mercies,
whom thou, in terms so bloody and so dear,
hast made thine enemies?

ANTONIO

Fair and gracious, Duke Orsino, noble sir,
Be pleased that I shake off these names you give me:
Antonio never yet was thief or pirate.
I am a simple man, law abiding, mostly.
I know not how, but witchcraft drew me hither.
That most ungrateful boy there by your side,
from the rude sea's enraged and foamy mouth
did I redeem; a wreck past hope he was.
His life I gave him and did thereto add my purse.
For his sake did I expose myself here,
into the danger of this adverse town;
drew to defend him when he was beset;
and for my pains was by him denied and
by your men arrested.

VIOLA

How can this be?

DUKE ORSINO

When came he to this town?

ANTONIO

Today, my lord, and for three months before,
was he with me, at my home, eating my food.

(Enter Olivia with Maria and Attendants.)

Act 5 Scene 1

DUKE ORSINO
Ah!
Here comes the countess, have we no music? No?
No matter. Now heaven walks on earth here. –
But for thee, fellow, thy words are madness:
three months this youth hath tended upon me;
but more of that anon. Take him aside. –
My darling, sweet Olivia, I am here.

OLIVIA
What would my lord, but that he may not have,
wherein Olivia may seem serviceable?
Cesario, you do not keep promise with me.

VIOLA
Madam!

DUKE ORSINO
Gracious Olivia –

OLIVIA
What do you say, Cesario? Good my lord –

VIOLA
My lord would speak; my duty hushes me.

OLIVIA
If it be aught to hold tune, my lord,
it is as fat and fulsome to mine ear
as howling after music.

Act 5 Scene 1

DUKE ORSINO
Still so cruel?

OLIVIA
Still so constant, lord.

DUKE ORSINO
What, to perverseness? You uncivil lady
to whose ingrate and inauspicious altars
my soul the faithfull'st offerings hath breathed out
that e'er devotion tendered! What shall I do?

OLIVIA
Even what it please my lord, as ever.

DUKE ORSINO
Why should I not, if all hope hath expired,
like to the Egyptian thief at point of death,
kill what I love? – A savage jealousy
that sometimes savors nobility. But hear me this:
since you to non-regardance cast my faith,
you push me to cast away your heart's desire.
For this my minion, whom I know you love,
and whom, by heaven I swear, I tender dearly,
him will I tear out of that cruel eye,
where he sits crowned in his master's spite.
(To Viola.)
Come, boy, with me; my thoughts are ripe in mischief.
I'll sacrifice the lamb that I do love,
to spite a raven's heart within a dove.

VIOLA
I go with you most willingly, my lord,
even to a thousand deaths.

OLIVIA
Where goes Cesario?

VIOLA
After him I love.

OLIVIA
Ay me, detested! How am I beguiled!

VIOLA
Who does beguile you? Who does do you wrong?

OLIVIA
Hast thou forget thyself? Is it so long?
Call forth the holy father.

DUKE ORSINO
Come. Away!

OLIVIA
Wither, my lord? Cesario, husband, stay!

DUKE ORSINO
Husband!

OLIVIA
Aye, husband: can he that deny?

Act 5 Scene 1

DUKE ORSINO
Her husband, sirrah!

VIOLA
No, my lord, not I.

OLIVIA
Thou knowest thou art.

SECOND OFFICER
My lord, your pardons prithee: this lady,
on our way here with captured pirate fiend,
did hold us up from reaching you for that we
she could count as witnesses to holy
matrimony with this same man beside you.

DUKE ORSINO
(To Viola.)
Oh, thou dissembling cub! My soul is breaking!
Farewell, and take her, but direct thy feet
where thou and I henceforth may never meet.

VIOLA
My lord, I do protest –

OLIVIA
Husband, come to me.

(Enter Sir Andrew and Feste.)

SIR ANDREW
For the love of God, a surgeon! Send one presently to Sir Toby.

OLIVIA
What's the matter?

SIR ANDREW
He has broke my head across and has given Sir Toby a bloody coxcomb, too; for the love of God, your help!

OLIVIA
Who has done this, Sir Andrew?

SIR ANDREW
The count's gentleman, one Cesario. We took him for a coward, but he's the very devil incardinate.

DUKE ORSINO
My gentleman, Cesario?

FESTE
Good sir, he's right there!

SIR ANDREW
'Swounds, here he is! You broke my head for nothing,
and that that I did, I was set on to do it by Sir Toby.

Act 5 Scene 1

VIOLA
Why do you speak to me?

FESTE
Oh, no ... sir. You cannot wiggle free.

(Enter Sir Toby, supported by Malvolio.)

SIR ANDREW
Here comes Sir Toby halting: you shall hear more.

DUKE ORSINO
How now, antique knight! How is't with you?

SIR TOBY
You can't keep a good man down; I'll be fine.

MALVOLIO
My lady! I've freed myself from horrid prison,
and coming here did find Sir Toby on the ground.
In exchange for my strong support, he hath
confessed to mischief, and apologized.

SIR TOBY
'Tis true, I did treat this fellow poorly.

MARIA
And I.

FESTE
And even I,

for 'twas I, Malvolio, who Sir Mompas played.

OLIVIA
An you've learned some humble humility,
'twill be good, Malvolio, to have you
back in your rightful place.

MALVOLIO
Madam.

DUKE ORSINO
This is too much! I scarcely know what's
happening! My God, what now?

(Enter Sebastian.)

SEBASTIAN
(To Olivia.)
I am sorry, madam, I have hurt your kinsman:
but, had it been the brother of my blood,
I must have done no less when challenged.
You throw a strange regard upon me, and by that
I do perceive it hath offended you;
pardon me, sweet one, even for the vows
we made each other but so recently.

DUKE ORSINO
One face, one voice, one habit, and two persons!

SEBASTIAN
Antonio! Oh, my dear Antonio!

Act 5 Scene 1

ANTONIO
Sebastian, are you?

SEBASTIAN
Doubt that, Antonio?

ANTONIO
How have you made division of yourself?
An apple, cleft in two, is not more twin
than these two creatures. Which is Sebastian?

OLIVIA
Most wonderful!

SEBASTIAN
Do I stand there? I never had a brother.
Who is this apparition who wears my face?
Of family I have no one. I had a sister,
whom the blind and hungry waves have devour'd.
Good sir, what kin are you to me?
What countryman? What name? What parentage?

VIOLA
Of Messaline: Sebastian was my father;
such a Sebastian was my brother too,
so went he suited to his watery tomb.
If spirits can assume both form and suit,
you come to fright us.

SEBASTIAN
A spirit I am indeed, but clad in flesh.

Were you a woman, as the rest goes even,
I should my tears let fall upon your cheek
and cry "Thrice welcome, drowned Viola!"

VIOLA

Then it is indeed thee, true Sebastian!
But hold,
Do not embrace me till each circumstance
of place, time, fortune, do cohere and jump.
(To Orsino.)
For, I am Viola, which to confirm
I'll bring you to a captain in this town,
where lie my maiden weeds; by whose gentle help
I was preserved from angry sea and brought
to serve and grow to love thee, noble count.
All the occurrence of my fortune since
hath been between this lady and this lord.

SEBASTIAN
(To Olivia.)
So comes it, lady, you have been mistook,
but you would have been married to a maid!
Nor are you therein, by my life, deceived;
you are betroth'd both to a maid and man.

DUKE ORSINO

Be not amazed. Right noble is the blood of
Sebastian of Messaline and these his kin.
If this be so, as yet the glass seems true,
I shall have share in this most happy wreck.
(To Viola.)
Boy, thou hast said to me a thousand times

Act 5 Scene 1

thou never shouldst love a woman, but that
that woman look'd like me.

VIOLA
All those sayings will I say again.

DUKE ORSINO
(Kneeling.)
Give me thy hand, for it seems love was here
before me all along. Your master quits you.
Here is my hand: you shall from this time be
your master's mistress.

VIOLA
Yes, and yes, ever more!

OLIVIA
A sister! I've always wanted a sister. You are she!

SIR TOBY
Sir Andrew, I fear this has ended bad for thou.

SIR ANDREW
(To Maria.)
Yay, but perhaps consolation be near.

SIR TOBY
What, ho! Hands off, good knight; those fertile
stomping grounds have I before thee mounted.

SIR ANDREW
But, what?

MARIA
'Tis truth, my lady. Me! My Lord, my Sir Toby,
and me was married yesterday.

OLIVIA
I give you good blessings, Cousin Maria.

DUKE ORSINO
(To Antonio.)
Now, back to you, sir. About your turn as pirate –

ANTONIO
Never, sir! In your fair and wonderful presence --

DUKE ORSINO
Tush, hold your tongue, too clever fox, for I am
in cheery mood, and absolve you of all so
that you, friend, may friend to these two still be.

ANTONIO
Good sir!

SEBASTIAN
Good cheer!

OLIVIA
Good honeymoon!

MARIA
Good idea!

Act 5 Scene 1

SIR TOBY
I'll drink to that!

DUKE ORSINO
Good love!

VIOLA
Good happy ending!

FESTE
(Aside.)
Make of this what you will.
It seems all is now peaceful in Illyria.

DUKE ORSINO
Music!
Let music be the food of love, and let it play on.
Fool, earn your keep!

FESTE
(Singing.)
"When that I was and a little tiny boy,
With hey, ho, the wind and the rain,
A foolish thing was but a toy,
For the rain, it raineth every day.

But when I came to man's estate,

(All.)
With hey, ho, the wind and the rain,

'Gainst knaves and thieves men shut their gate,

(All.)
For the rain, it raineth every day.

But when I came, alas! to wive,

(All.)
With hey, ho, the wind and the rain.

By swaggering could I never thrive,

(All.)
For the rain, it raineth every day.

But when I came unto my beds,

(All.)
With hey, ho, the wind and the rain,

The toss-pots still had drunken heads,

(All.)
For the rain, it raineth every day.

A great while ago the world begun,

(All.)
With hey, ho, the wind and the rain,

But that's all one, our play is done,

(All.)
And we'll strive to please you every day."

EPILOGUE

Feste steps forward.

FESTE
Those of you with clever ears and sharpful minds
will recall I trust without too much prodding,
that after all this love and comedic times
I told you would come a time for applauding.
My lords, 'tis now.

CURTAINS

Character Notes

You've been cast! Hoorah! Now, before fame and glory, roses and candy, steak and cast parties, you must get to work. This is a lighthearted comedy, and therefore fairly simple to perform, but as anyone whose done comedy knows … it's all about

timing. You must know your lines rock solid, in order to deliver and make the most of your timing.

The play is written in iambic pentameter (look it up!), and the rhythm of the dialogue is part of its beauty. The trick is to learn it, get it down, and then make it work for you instead of remaining slave to it: breaking the rhythm is just important as keeping it … it's all about that timing. For example, Olivia's confession of love (Act 3 Scene 1) is in prose; she is too distraught and thrown off her usual game to continue in verse. (Fortunately, for you, this "Do Able" version has taken pains to make the language flow easily, even to our modern ears; if you're curious about the changes, compare this to the original play and you'll quickly understand.)

As mentioned, this is a light comedy. Shakespeare having fun. The 12th night title refers to the final day in the season of Christmas, where holiday parties are at their climax. For themes, we have the overpowering drive of erotic love, and the impermanence of life. It's the 1600's version of "Don't worry, be happy."

The following character notes are meant as a starting point, to help you understand your character. Find what you can here, and then look elsewhere, everywhere, even inside yourself, to find more. Anything that can help you bring these fun characters to life.

VIOLA – One of, if not the all time best Shakespearian heroine. She is all girl, meaning she's loving, sensitive and understanding, but at the same time strong and capable; do not think of her as any sort of timid wall flower. She is not a fighter, no doubt because she was not trained to swordfight like her brother, Sebastian, clearly was, growing up. But she is no coward and does not back down from conflicts. Note how quickly she steps up to support Duke Orsino at the end, even when it means her death!

Much is said about twins, how they think alike. Viola and Sebastian are very much alike. They both have oodles of charm and intellect, able to talk their way out of almost anything.

Viola is educated, clearly. That is a mark of her fine family background. That her father knew of the Duke Orsino also shows that her family is of some high standing. Duke Orsino quickly agrees to marry her, after learning her family is noble (and of course, after finding out she's not a guy!).

Focus on loyalty, too. Viola goes the extra mile trying to woo Olivia for the Duke. Valentine, even though he's a gentleman and presumably also loyal to Duke Orsino, gave up much easier.

SEBASTIAN – Hero type. Although not in the whole play, he comes in as the dashing swashbuckler to save the day. He's also a bit of an opportunist, isn't he? Though he doesn't understand why Olivia is so hot for him, he doesn't hesitate to take her up on her offered love.

He is noble, and accordingly follows through with his promise (and presumably then makes a good husband for Olivia).

DUKE ORSINO

– Love's besotted fool? Yes, though not an idiot. He is melancholy. He is very driven by his desires, so much so that he is blind and deaf to Olivia's refusals, and blind in not seeing that he has Viola's love from the beginning.

He seems a fair enough ruler, though distracted by love, and not exactly involved in running his dukedom. As a younger man he must have been more involved, since he was on a ship that saw pirate action (attack by Antonio) and remembers it well.

He's a perfect gentleman: handsome, brave, noble, in control, rich and powerful. Presumably, this is what makes Viola love him.

OLIVIA

– Like Duke Orsino, she seems more focused on herself than on affairs of state. Her seven-year mourning period is dropped immediately (in fact, we hear no more of it) after she meets Viola (as Cesario). Just like the Duke, Olivia lets her hormones rule her actions.

Smart, even crafty (for example, sending the ring with Malvolio). Scheming. But honest and steadfast, too: she doesn't, for example, lead Orsino on when it would have been so easy to do so, and once she wins Cesario (really Sebastian), she follows through to marriage.

FESTE

Are you to play Feste! Oh, hang on tight! What a fun role!

Feste breaks the fourth wall. He plays with the audience, in addition to playing with other characters. There's a bit of singing, and it would help if you can strum a harp (or play some other instrument), plus dance around freely. While physical stunts are not called for in the script, this is a role that easily allows (even encourages) whatever hijinks you can bring.

Super witty – Robin Williams level. Feste is smarter than the other characters. But he recognizes his place in life, and accepts his role.

SIR TOBY

Rascal to the end, almost. He gets away with lots, counting on his status as Olivia's kin, and he freeloads off of Sir Andrew's money. Drunk, playboy, cheater.

But he redeems himself by first recognizing that their prank against Malvolio goes too far, and second by marrying Maria. There is hope for him in the end. And he gets beat up by Sebastian, so that's a bit of penalty to convince him to continue mending his ways.

Sir Toby is a corrupt knight, interested mostly in serving himself with excessive eating, drinking and whoring. He takes advantage of his "friend" Sir Andrew without any touch of conscience. But he is a lovable rogue, and serves as comic relief – not villain.

SIR ANDREW

– Unfortunately, the big loser of the play. Invited in on false pretenses (the idea that Olivia would ever accept his love), he funds Sir Toby's extravagances, gets talked into staying long after he wanted to cut and run, and then gets beaten up in the end by Sebastian – and still doesn't get the girl.

Apparently, he goes off home at the end, with nothing to show for his time in Illyria. He's been cheated, and doesn't seem to even recognize it.

He's not very bright, or he would have seen how Sir Toby abuses him. He likes to think he is a loyal and steadfast knight, but he's more coward than such words would imply. Point in fact:

Sebastian beats both Sir Andrew and Sir Toby, at the same time, and Sebastian doesn't have a scratch to show for the encounter!

MARIA – Gentlewoman, i.e. companion of Olivia. Some scripts say "maid" but even if she is the housekeeper, she is more than maid. She's at Olivia's side often. Which is likely why she and butler Malvolio clash – a struggle for Olivia's affection, and power over the household.

Maria is smart. And where other characters are silly head-over-heels chasing love, Maria is practical about it. She likes Sit Toby, and gets him, with no fuss.

She gets Toby, in part, by impressing him with her devious prank against Malvolio. Sir Toby admires a good con!

MALVOLIO – The foil to almost every other character, he is the direct opposite of the merrymaking duo of Sirs Toby and Andrew. The others are whimsy, chasing love in madcap fashion. Malvolio is dark, humorless.

Malvolio's ego is his downfall. He is obsessed with power, control over the household. The moment he finds what he thinks is Olivia's love letter, he immediately thinks he would be a good match for her. Then he shows how stupid and blind love can be.

ANTONIO

What a character! He can be downplayed as just a bystander who happened to find Sebastian on the beach (as Viola was pulled out by the Captain), or he can be played much larger, as Sebastian's true friend. He even professes love for Sebastian, and it would not be a stretch to add that Antonio is gay (and even, perhaps, that Sebastian is bi).

Antonio is a rogue, but loveable. A pirate – possibly redeemed, though it's unclear what he does now.

He's educated, and likely from a similar background as Sebastian: nobility of some sort. Has he fallen?

Set Design Notes

Film versions of *Twelfth Night* are free to use the seashore and various town and castle settings, but of course on stage one is limited to sets. The play is quite easily done on a minimalistic set, and indeed in Shakespeare's time of traveling actors, often there was no set at all.

What set you can build may depend upon what you have. Your space. Your budget. Your available materials. Your time. Your skill level. Your ready help. It's always best to start by recognizing what you have already.

The set for *Twelfth Night* can be big or small, but it must meet certain needs. Let's list those first, so that sets can be designed first for purpose and second for art:

- Beach – perhaps just a backdrop and some

Production Notes

  seagull sounds?
  - Act 1 Scene 2 – Viola's entrance
  - Act 2 Scene 1 – Sebastian's entrance

- Duke Orsino's palace – a lounge type space, with room for musicians, lords and court attendants.
  - Act 1 Scene 1
  - Act 1 Scene 4
  - Act 2 Scene 4

- Olivia's place – multiple spaces:
  - Act 1 Scene 3 – inside the house
  - Act 1 Scene 5 – inside the house
  - Act 2 Scene 3 – inside the house
  - Act 2 Scene 5 – garden
  - Act 3 Scene 1 – garden
  - Act 3 Scene 2 – inside the house
  - Act 3 Scene 4 – garden
  - Act 4 Scene 1 – in front of house
  - Act 4 Scene 2 – inside the house
  - Act 4 Scene 3 – garden
  - Act 5 Scene 1 – in front of the house

- Street – outside
  - Act 2 Scene 2 – the ring
  - Act 3 Scene 3 – Sebastian arrives

Production License

Shakespeare's play is in the public domain, but this version of it has been created by Brent Nautic Von Horn, who holds all copyright and all rights to performance. (Though, of course, no rights are claimed to Shakespeare's characters and words.)

All rights to perform *Doable Twelfth Night's* version of *Twelfth Night* on stage for a live audience will be granted to you, almost free of charge, provided:

> 1. you request a license to use this work from the author at the following email address:
>
> nauticproductions@yahoo.com

2. you (or your production) purchase at least ten (10) or more copies of the hardcopy paperback version of this book *Doable Twelfth Night* from the author (you'll need at least 10 copies of the script for your actors)

3. you send at least 3 pictures of your production to the author's email address above; <u>and</u>

4. that you give credit to the author (Brent Nautic Von Horn) and the book *Doable Twelfth Night* in some nice manner (preferably in your play's program, though on your poster or even in sky writing would be real nice, too)

ALL OTHER RIGHTS are expressly retained by the author, including (without limitation) all rights to film, record, broadcast, stream, or present this work in any manner other than a live performance as above.